JONNY LAMBERT'S

Bear and Bird
Explore the Seashore

CAN YOU SPOT?

Mussels

Seashells

WHAT TO SPOT

Use the "CAN YOU SPOT?" panels on every page to discover seashore secrets as you join Bear and Bird on their beach adventure.

What kind of shell has Bear found?

CAN YOU HELP?

Can you help Bear and Bird find what they are looking for?

For everyone who loves exploring at the beach —Jonny Lambert

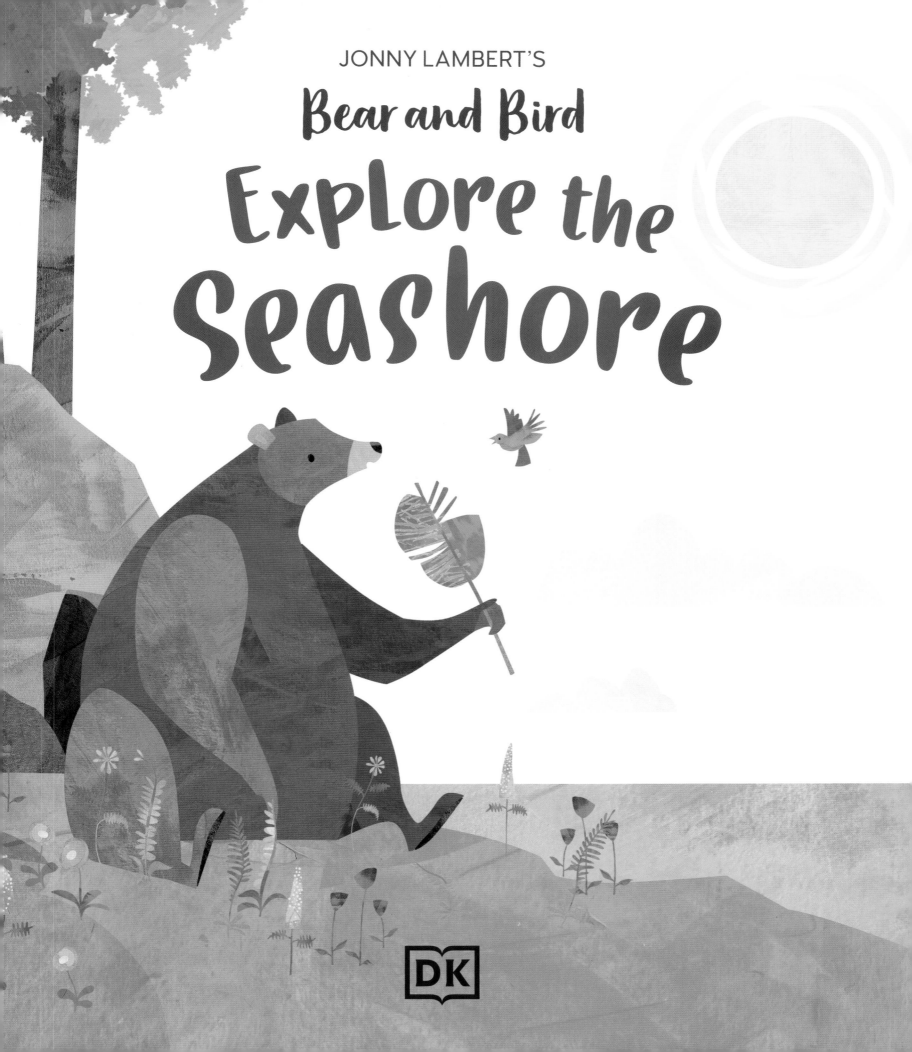

JONNY LAMBERT'S

Bear and Bird

Explore the

Seashore

DK

On a hot, sunny morning, Bear and Bird decide to go to the beach and paddle at the water's edge.

Bear's excited! Setting off with Bird, he puts on his big, floppy hat and says, "We could build sandcastles!"

What is Moose sitting in?

CAN YOU SPOT?

Hat

Bucket

Shovel

Sailboat

Sun

CAN YOU SPOT?

Pebbles

Waves

Cloud

Marram grass

Red valerian

When Bear and Bird arrive, it's high tide—the water has covered the sand.

Bear's not happy.
"I can't build pebble castles!" he says.

Bird suggests they explore instead.
"Let's go beachcombing!
We won't disturb any creatures
and we'll leave things on the
beach when we've finished."

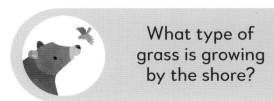

What type of
grass is growing
by the shore?

Splashing along the water's edge,
Bear and Bird spot their first beach find.

Glistening among the
pebbles are empty abalone shells.

What kind
of shell has
Bear found?

The wet, silvery-white surfaces sparkle like jewels.

Gulls swoop to see what they have found.

CAN YOU SPOT?

Rock

Abalone shell

Gull

Seaweed

CAN YOU SPOT?

Mussels

Seashells

Barnacles

Sea urchin shell

Whelk

As they clamber over some large rocks, the mussels and barnacles are sharp on Bear's soft paws.

But they continue to find more beautiful seashells in different colors, shapes, and sizes.

Bear picks up a round sea urchin shell.

Can you find a fish?

CAN YOU SPOT?

Shrimp

Sea anemone

Lobster

Starfish

Common goby

Next the friends peer into a tide pool.

Sea anemone tentacles sway, shrimp scurry, and a small fish darts back and forth.

Bear sees something glinting
in the water. Being very careful,
he leans forward to get a closer look.

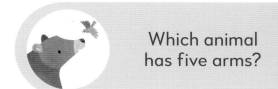

Which animal
has five arms?

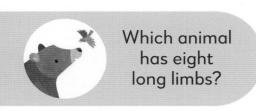
Which animal has eight long limbs?

Bear reaches down to retrieve the glinting blue sea glass.

Bird spies a hermit crab, scuttling along the tide pool floor.

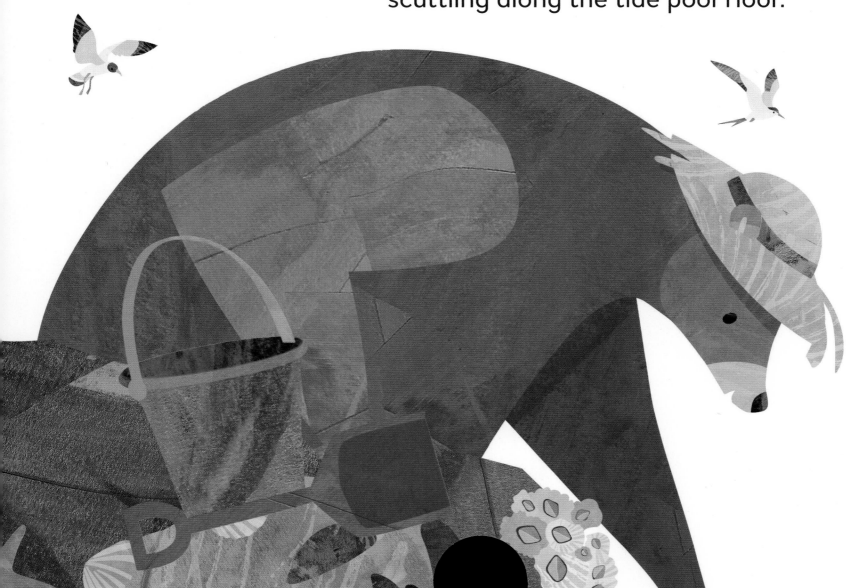

"Wow! That crab's carrying its home on its back!" says Bird.

Bear laughs. "I'm not strong enough to carry the cave that's our home!"

CAN YOU SPOT?

Sea glass

Hermit crab

Octopus

Clams

Jellyfish

As Bear sits to admire his blue glass jewel, he notices Bird's perch is moving slowly toward the sea.

Which fish has a horse-shaped head?

CAN YOU SPOT?

Seahorse

Oyster

Scallop

Coral

Razor clams

Bear is puzzled. He says, "Bird, you're standing on a funny looking rock that's moving down the beach!"

Shore crab

CAN YOU SPOT?

Fishing net

Loggerhead
turtle

Mooring buoy

It turns out that Bird is on the back
of a loggerhead turtle!

But around the turtle's neck
hangs a discarded fishing net.

Bear and Bird carefully free the turtle
from her unwanted burden.

Free from the fishing net, the turtle makes her way into the surf.

Bear mutters, "Garbage like this shouldn't be on the beach!"
And he promptly stuffs the net into his bucket so he can take it away.

CAN YOU SPOT?

Pebbles with holes in them

Polished pebbles

Plaice

What was hanging around the turtle's neck?

CAN YOU SPOT?

Cormorant

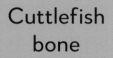

Cuttlefish
bone

Dolphin

Island

Mackerel

In the bay, dolphin play, leaping high
and slapping the water.

Bear and Bird rest by the shore
and watch them.

As water ripples around Bear's feet, he
picks up a cuttlefish bone from the beach.

"Yummy!" chirps Bird excitedly.
"I love to eat cuttlefish bones!"

Bear is about to reply when...

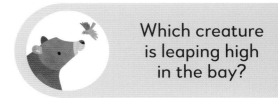

Which creature is leaping high in the bay?

a cormorant appears, hops on a rock,
and gulps down a shiny mackerel.

"Now, that's yummy!" says Bear.

CAN YOU SPOT?

Ammonite

Cliff

Seal

Gannet

Tern

Bear and Bird walk along the shore. They stop to look at a very peculiar shell shape in a rock.

"Look, Bird! This shell is stuck in the rock," says Bear.

"I think it must be the remains of a creature from a long time ago," says Bird. "Let's leave it where we found it."

"I agree," replies Bear. "We don't want to break anything."

What type of fossil shell did Bear and Bird see in a rock?

Among the rocks, Bear finds some pieces of wood.
"Look! Wibbly, wobbly sticks!" he says.

What tall building can you see on a rock?

Bird explains the sticks are called driftwood.
They have probably drifted in the ocean for many years.

Bear is amazed by the driftwood shapes.

"Ha, ha! And this one looks like me dancing!" he exclaims.

CAN YOU SPOT?

Orca

Lighthouse

Driftwood

Fish bones

What is Moose flying?

"Look!" chirps Bird excitedly. "The tide is going out!"

Bear and Bird hurry back along the shore.
Bear is eager to build his sandcastle.

CAN YOU SPOT?

Sand

Sea

Footprint

Worm cast

Kite

But as Bear lays out their beach finds
on the sand, he has an idea.
"Let's make a picture instead!"

And that's what they did!

What did we see along the seashore?

Abalone shell

Sea urchin shell

Common goby

Hat

Waves

Gull

Whelk

Sea glass

Bucket

Cloud

Shrimp

Hermit crab

Shovel

Seaweed

Sea anemone

Octopus

Sailboat

Marram grass

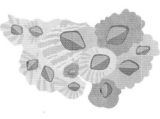

Mussels

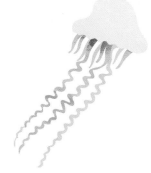

Clams

Sun

Red valerian

Seashells

Lobster

Pebbles

Rock

Barnacles

Starfish

Jellyfish

Seahorse

Fishing net

Cormorant

Seal

Fish bones

Oyster

Loggerhead turtle

Gannet

Sand

Scallop

Mooring buoy

Dolphin

Tern

Sea

Coral

Pebbles with holes in them

Island

Orca

Footprint

Polished pebbles

Mackerel

Lighthouse

Worm cast

Razor clams

Plaice

Ammonite

Shore crab

Cuttlefish bone

Cliff

Driftwood

Kite

DK | Penguin Random House

Illustrated and written by Jonny Lambert
Senior Editor Dawn Sirett
US Senior Editor Shannon Beatty
Designer Eleanor Bates
Senior Production Editor Nikoleta Parasaki
Production Controller Leanne Burke
Managing Editor Penny Smith
Deputy Art Director Mabel Chan
Publisher Francesca Young
Publishing Director Sarah Larter

First American Edition, 2024
Published in the United States by DK Publishing
1745 Broadway, 20th Floor, New York, NY 10019

Copyright © 2024 Dorling Kindersley Limited
DK, a Division of Penguin Random House LLC
24 25 26 27 28 10 9 8 7 6 5 4 3 2 1
001–337240–Mar/2024

A catalog record for this book
is available from the Library of Congress.
ISBN: 978-0-7440-9189-2

DK books are available at special discounts when purchased
in bulk for sales promotions, premiums, fund-raising, or
educational use. For details, contact:
DK Publishing Special Markets,
1745 Broadway, 20th Floor, New York, NY 10019
SpecialSales@dk.com

Printed and bound in China

www.dk.com

MIX
Paper | Supporting
responsible forestry
FSC™ C018179

This book was made with Forest
Stewardship Council™ certified
paper—one small step in DK's
commitment to a sustainable future.
For more information go to
www.dk.com/our-green-pledge